Patriotic Solos
Primer Level

Compiled and Arranged by Wesley Schaum

Foreword

This book is designed to make familiar patriotic music easy to play. A student with just six to eight weeks study could start enjoying this album.

The pieces are arranged with melody divided between hands in five-finger position. A minimum of finger numbers is used. Large notes and spacious music notation help make music reading easier.

Duet accompaniments offer many possibilities for recitals, school assemblies and scout events. The duets help provide valuable rhythmic training and ensemble experience especially valuable to beginners. The duets are recommended for use at home as well as at the lesson. The person playing the accompaniment is free to add pedal according to his/her own taste.

Contents

EXCLUSIVELY DISTRIBUTED BY

HAL•LEONARD® CORPORATION

7777 W. BLUEMOUND RD. P.O. BOX 13819 MILWAUKEE, WI 53213

ISBN-13: 978-1-936098-91-0

Duet Accompaniment

Notes with stems UP are to be played with the *right* hand. Notes with stems DOWN are for the *left* hand.

Teacher's Note: If the pupil is in the early grades in school and has not yet had fractions, it may be better NOT to try explaining the dotted quarter notes and 8th notes. Instead, teach the rhythm by rote. Explain this rhythm at a later time when the student has learned fractions.

Marine's Hymn

Allegro

Traditional

4

Duet Accompaniment

America

M. Henry Carey
Words by Samuel F. Smith

Duet Accompaniment

Yankee Doodle

Giocoso

Traditional

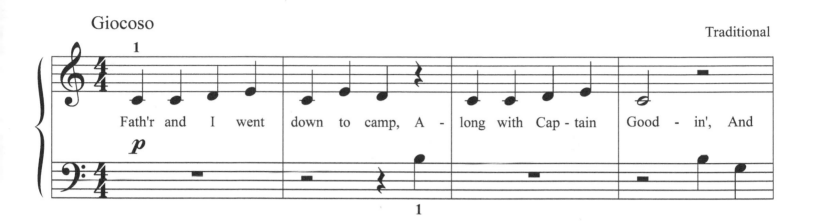

Fath'r and I went down to camp, A - long with Cap - tain Good - in', And

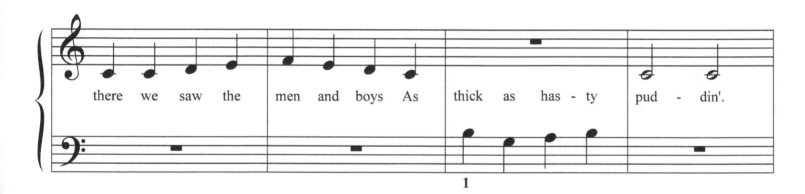

there we saw the men and boys As thick as has - ty pud - din'.

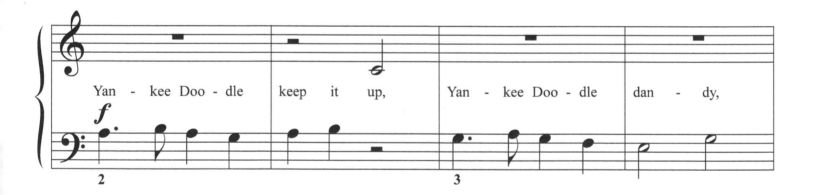

Yan - kee Doo - dle keep it up, Yan - kee Doo - dle dan - dy,

Mind the mu - sic and the step, And with the girls be han - dy.

Battle Hymn of the Republic

William Steffe
Words by Julia Ward Howe

Maestoso

Duet Accompaniment

Teacher's Note: If desired, the 8th notes may be played in "swing style" for more authentic rhythm.

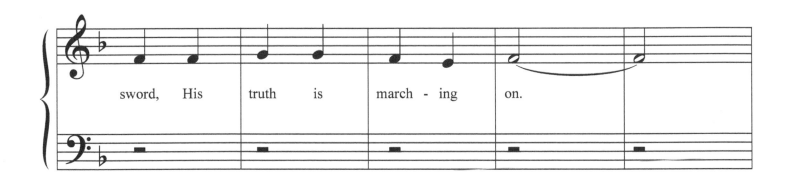

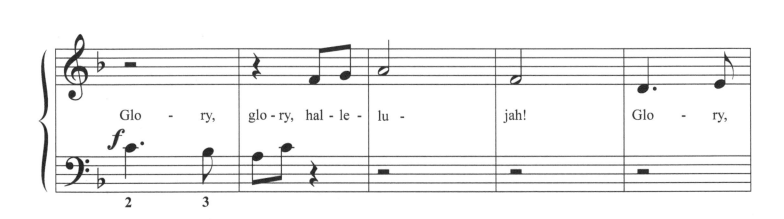

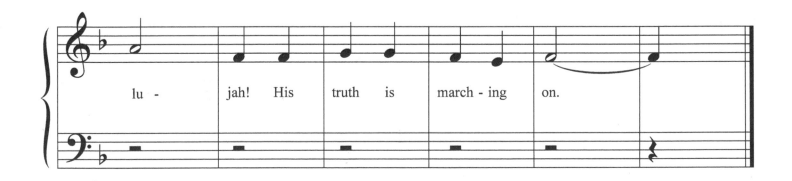

Duet Accompaniment

Anchors Aweigh

Charles A. Zimmerman
Words revised by John W. Schaum

Caissons' Song

Words and Music by Edmund L. Gruber

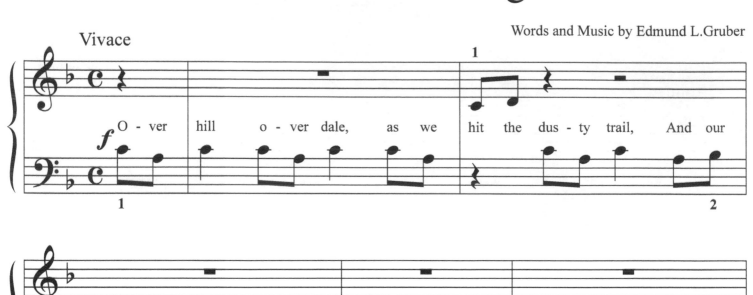

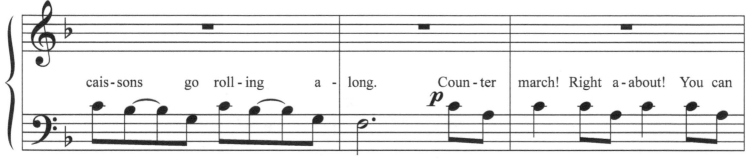

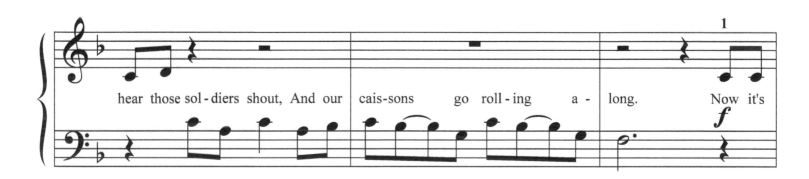

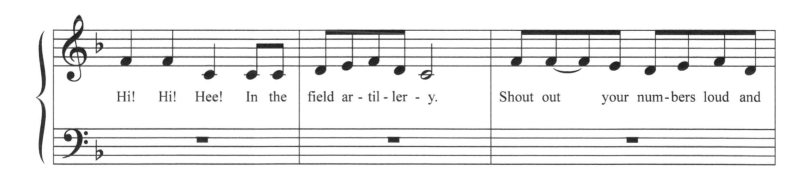

Duet Accompaniment

strong! Where e'er we go, you will al - ways know that those

cais - sons go roll-ing a - long. That those cais-sons go roll-ing a - long.

Caissons (KAY-sahns) are wagons used to carry ammunition for army artillery (cannons and other large guns). Caissons were originally pulled by horses and, in the early 1900's, by trucks. However, the modern army no longer uses caissons. The music has become the official song of the U.S. Army.

Duet Accompaniment

America the Beautiful

Samuel Augustus Ward
Words by Katherine Lee Bates

You're a Grand Old Flag

Words and music by
George M. Cohan

Spiritoso

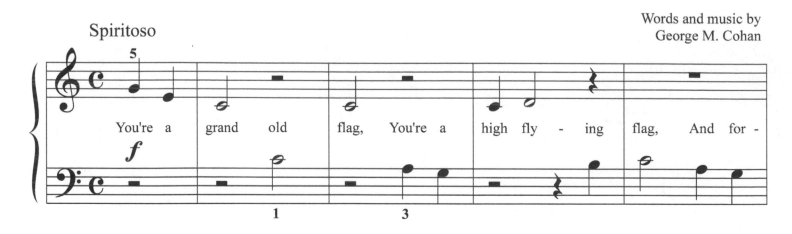

You're a grand old flag, You're a high fly - ing flag, And for -

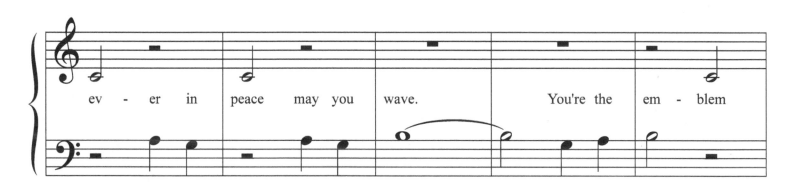

ev - er in peace may you wave. You're the em - blem

of the land I love, The home of the free and the

Duet Accompaniment

brave. Ev - 'ry heart beats true, Un - der Red, White and Blue, where there's

p

3

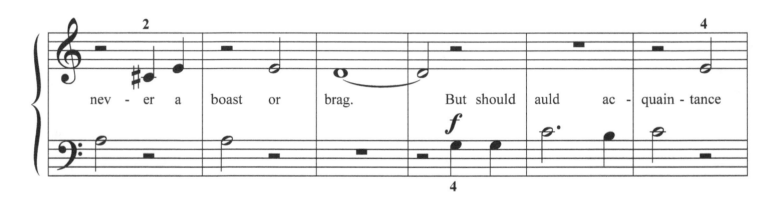

nev - er a boast or brag. But should auld ac - quain - tance

f

2

4

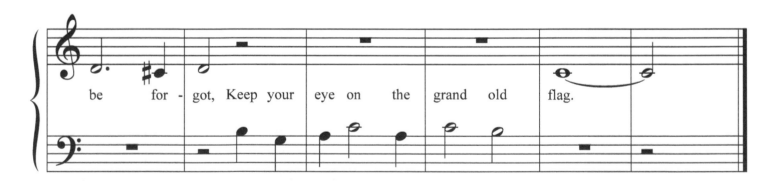

be for - got, Keep your eye on the grand old flag.

Stars and Stripes Forever

Words and music by
John Philip Sousa

Alla marcia

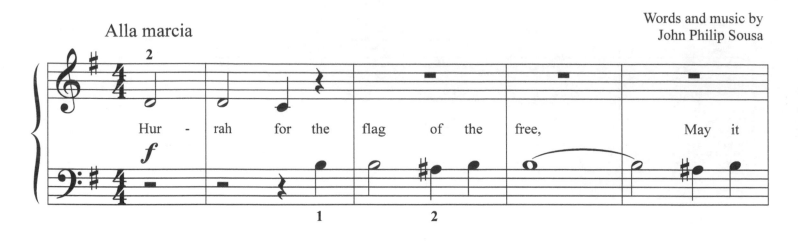

Hur - rah for the flag of the free, May it

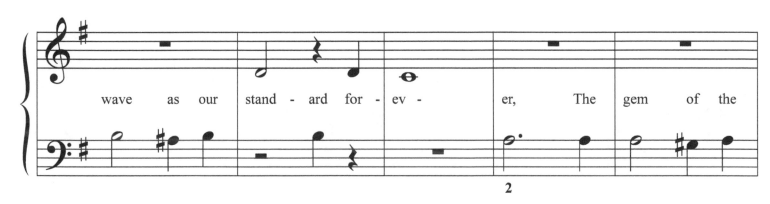

wave as our stand - ard for - ev - er, The gem of the

land and the sea, The___ ban - ner of the

Duet Accompaniment

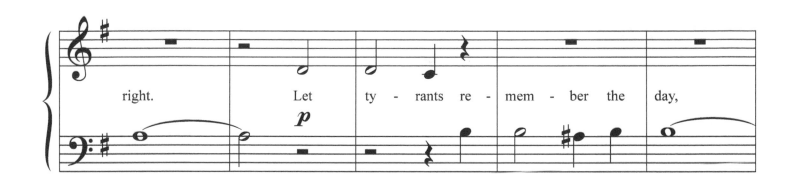

right.　　Let　ty - rants re - mem - ber the day,

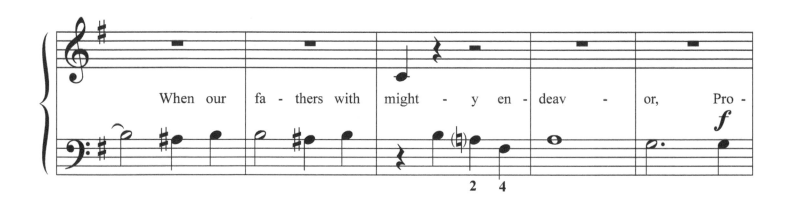

When our fa - thers with might - y en - deav - or, Pro -

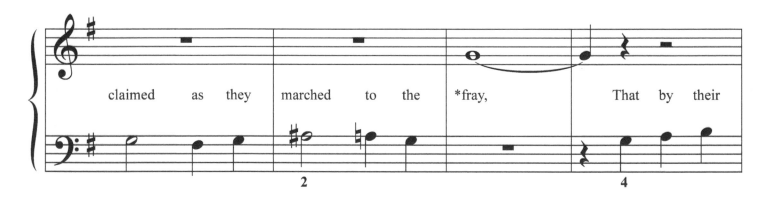

claimed as they marched to the *fray,　That by their

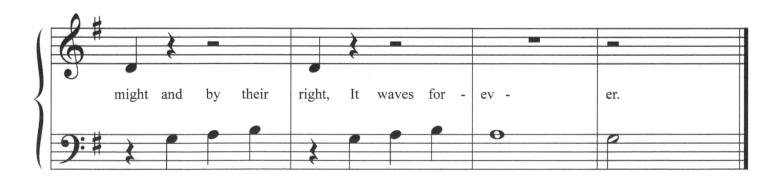

might and by their right, It waves for - ev - er.

* **Fray** means a fight or battle.

Hail to the Chief

James Sanderson
Words by Sir Walter Scott

Hail to the chief who in tri - umph ad - van - ces,

Hon - ored and bless'd be the ev - er - green_ pine! Long may the tree, in his

ban - ner that glan - ces, Flou - rish the shel - ter and

grace of our line! Hail to the chief who in tri - umph ad - van - ces,

Duet Accompaniment

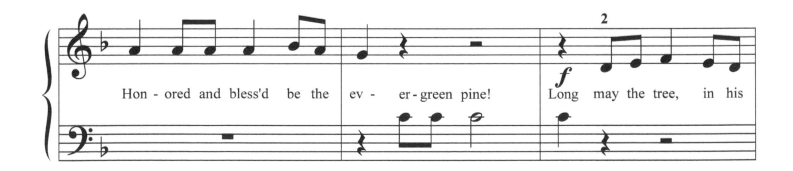

Hon - ored and bless'd be the ev - er - green pine! Long may the tree, in his ban - ner that glan - ces, Flou - rish the shel - ter and grace of our line!

This is the official march of the President of the United States. It is performed by military bands when the President appears for a formal visit and for official government ceremonies.

Star Spangled Banner

John Stafford Smith
Words by Francis Scott Key

Duet Accompaniment